ROCKET
FANTASTIC

ALSO BY GABRIELLE CALVOCORESSI

APOCALYPTIC SWING

THE LAST TIME I SAW AMELIA EARHART

ROCKET

FANTASTIC

POEMS

GABRIELLE

CALVOCORESSI

A KAREN & MICHAEL BRAZILLER BOOK

PERSEA BOOKS

NEW YORK

Persea Books, Inc.
277 Broadway
New York, New York 10007

Library of Congress Cataloging-in-Publication Data

Names: Calvocoressi, Gabrielle, author.
Title: Rocket fantastic : poems / Gabrielle Calvocoressi.
Description: New York, New York : Persea Books Inc., [2017]
Identifiers: LCCN 2017013416 I ISBN 9780892554850 (hardcover : alk. paper)
Classification: LCC PS3603.A4465 A6 2017 I DDC 811/.6—dc23
LC record available at https://lccn.loc.gov/2017013416

Book design and composition by Rita Lascaro
Typeset in Janson
Manufactured in the United States of America. Printed on acid-free paper.

Thomas, Lisa, & Ameya Calvocoressi
&
Ellen Bryant Voigt & Gabriel Fried

For making the world that made my voice. And for helping me go find it.

CONTENTS

ACKNOWLEDGMENTS

Grateful acknowledgment is given to the publications in which these poems, in some form, appeared: The Academy of American Poets' "Poem A Day", *Alaska Quarterly Review, American Poetry Review, The Awl, Boston Review, CURA, Gulf Coast, Kenyon Review, Kenyon Review Online, Ploughshares, Poetry, The Poetry Review, Provincetown Arts, New England Review, The New York Times/T Magazine, The Rumpus.*

"She Ties My Bow Tie" appeared on Poetry Daily.

"I Was Popular in Certain Circles" was included in *Environmental and Nature Writing: A Writer's Guide and Anthology* from Bloomsbury Press.

For the gift of time, shelter, and financial support, I am endlessly grateful to Civitella di Ranieri Foundation and The Lannan Foundation, specifically Dana Prescott, Diego Mencaroni, Martha Jessup, Douglas Humble, and the wonderful people of Marfa, Texas. And to my brother Kevin McGann and his family for time by the ocean and the gift of being found by them.

Thanks to my remarkable colleagues and friends at UNC Chapel Hill and The Program For Writers at Warren Wilson College. And to my students who are also my teachers. Thanks also to the wonderful people at Indiana University, The Fine Arts Work Center and The Vermont Studio Center for your ears, hearts and inspiration as I experimented with these poems.

Thanks to Tom Lutz, Jonathan Hahn, Evan Kindley, Michael Ursell, Elizabeth Metzger, and Joshua Rivkin at *Los Angeles Review of Books.* You taught me more about poetry than I ever thought possible.

Thanks to Kimberly Witherspoon and the folks at Inkwell Management for taking such good care. You are the best.

For friendship, love and loyalty beyond words, I am grateful to David Adjmi, Kaveh Akbar, Nadia Benamara, Jared Brown, Michael and Karen Braziller, Damon Dorsey, Romayne Rubinas Dorsey, Pam Durban, Robin Ekiss, Jonathan Farmer, Vievee Francis, Ross Gay, Marianne Gingher, Matthew Grady, Stephanie Elizondo Griest, francine j harris. Tom Healy and Fred Hochberg, Jennifer Ho, A. Van Jordan, Randall Kenan, Heidi Kim, Dana Levin, Jenny Lind, Art Lyons, Adrian Matejka, Michael McFee, Michael Mekeel, Ian Morse, Frances Offenhauser, Matthew Olzmann, Peter Perlman, Daniel Pipski, Alex Raben, Evan Rhodes, Martha Rhodes, Michelle Robinson, Miguel Sapochnik, Alan Shapiro, Bland Simpson, Heather Taylor and Alex de Cordoba, Yoshi Shaka, Helina Shaka, Daniel Wallace, Laura Wallace, Crystal Williams, Ross White, and Erin Zimring.

To Richard Howard, for knowing where to lead me long ago.

For the longest dearest friendship and the perfect home to write in, my thanks to Amy G. Lehman and Max Lehman. My life and this book is better because of you.

To Jennifer Chang. For being such a good friend for so long. For being the best.

To Gabriel Fried. For trusting me and telling me and being the most incredible friend, editor, and collaborator for almost two decades now. My growth as an artist would be impossible without you making space for me to fail and figure it out and find out where words could lead me.

And to Angeline. For everything. Everything. Always.

A NOTE FOR THE READER

The symbol ⚧ is used as a pronoun in *Rocket Fantastic* when referring to the figure of the Bandleader. It represents a confluence of genders in varying degrees, not either/or nor necessarily both in equal measure. It is simultaneously encompassing and fluctuating, pronounced by me with the intake of breath when a body is unlimited in its possibilities.

ROCKET
FANTASTIC

Shave

Like the buck I am I turn my head
side to side. I hear the leaves
rustle. I shake my head a little
and birds reel 'round the forest.
I am no branch. My head turns
to the side. I see out my side
eye. The deep pool of the eye
sees itself pool in the mirror.
I oil myself 'til I am all a lather.
My chest heaves out
so my full heart can abandon
the ribs' stockade. Where
the bullet would go if the hunter
were a good shot: that's
where I place the razor.
I make my skin taut. I pull
my own neck back and to
the side. I come for myself.
Yes, I was a lady once but now
I take the blade and move it
slowly past the jugular, up
the ridge of my chin where
the short hairs glisten. I was
once ashamed. It was a thing
I did in private. My own self
my quarry. No more.
Look how the doe comes 'round
and also the doves and also
the wolf who lets me pass.
The fox offers me the squirrel's
hide to buff myself to shining.
There is no such thing except
the smoothness of my face.

There's a point where it all gets still,

        when the Bandleader's there between the branches

of my fingers. When I cover my eyes

        as if to block ℁ out. To the left of us,

to the left of the city an hour away,

        there's the place my father called

the null point:

        where you can see better and everything gets

like a spring morning, he'd stand

        behind us on the mountain. He'd place

his hands on my shoulders.

        He'd say, *Try it*

with the birds first, my thumb in the early light

surrounded by golden haze. I'd cover

the bird no larger than

my thumb. Then we'd find the locusts

and then we'd try the bees

(the day growing hotter, the day itself starting

to hum and buzz). Get still,

he'd say, Let your eyes get loose and

double. And then focus in.

To the left. To the spot the summer came inside

me. Still and silent like someone diving in the pool.

How you lie there in the stillness 'til they

surface. That's how we learned. Birds then the bees

then the mayflies like dandelions blown to

bits. I was better at it than my Brother.

I was more patient: little thumb on the mayfly,

little thumb held to the left of us.

The Sun Got All Over Everything

Over the boys and girls by the pool,
over the bougainvillea, which got so hot
my palms stayed warm for minutes after.
It made a mess of a day
that was supposed to be the worst
and lured me outside so I forgot her death entirely.
And also the polar bears scrambling
on the ice chips. And also that there was no water
in the Golden State. The pool was full
and the sun poured across the women's bodies
so you had to shade your eyes. Or I did. I had to
put my hand up to see what they were saying.
I know it's no excuse. And I had made a plan
to cry all day

and into the evening. I marked in my book,
which seems like something I'd make up in a poem
except this time I actually did it.
I wrote: *Grieve.* Because we're all so busy
aren't we? And so broke. I needed to make
an appointment with my anguish, so I could
take my mind off buying groceries
that I really couldn't afford. Anyway.
I didn't mean to go outside except there
the sky was, just ridiculously blue,
taunting me with pigment that I felt
the need to name. And from somewhere
close by a voice I couldn't see because the sun
was like a yolk cracked over it said,

What are you drinking? And I said,
I'm grieving. I'm very busy remembering.

*I made an appointment because last year
I forgot and then felt awful.* The sun opened
its mouth and made a gong of the canyons.

It poured across the girls and slicked across
their Dior lenses. I put my tongue on it
exactly when I should have been tearing
at my clothes and lighting candles.
I got on top and let it find the tightness
in my back and open where my wings would
be. Somewhere my mother was dying
and someone was skinning a giraffe.
And I let it go. I just let it go.

I remember Dad would tell us the story of Isaac though I never knew why but sort of like a lesson and a joke and we should be grateful all in one. I remember thinking about how it took three days. A three day hump we'd say here. That's a long time. That's long enough to know and want to go back and know you're not going back anytime soon. I remember saying that to Dad how long that was. And he'd say, *It's not so long if you know you're right.* I remember him saying that and thinking, *Right about what?* Three days is long enough that everything gets so wet you're five pounds heavier just from sweat it's long enough that your feet stop hurting and just get numb. And he was just a *boy*, though that's when he'd tell the story, wasn't it? When we were walking into camp and we'd be tired and he'd say, Isaac walked for three whole days and sometimes he'd kind of sing it, *Isaac walked for three whole days!* And I'd hate him then I'll say that now I hated him then and thought he was a vicious man. In his windbreaker and collared shirt taking us up to see the stars. You never seemed to mind, you'd sing too sometimes. Isaac walked for three whole days. And I'd say, *Some bargain.* And he'd stop and look me level in the eye and say, *Well young man, no one says you have to make it back.*

※'s huge. Standing there in the woods

where I didn't even see whose at first.

※ doesn't know I'm looking.

※ moves a little bit and kicks the ground.

I was walking by myself as the sun set.

I kept going in deeper to the greenest
spot until I found a clearing.

※ was the clearing.

※ took the clearing up and stood there
still and watched me 'til I saw whose.

I saw whose shoulders first and then whose neck.

I think ※ was so golden in the sun I
didn't know what ※ was. And I thought:

the branches were whose horns.

I thought ℅ was an eight point stag.

And how whose chest made a kind of giant heart out of me

out of my eyes looking.

And ℅ let me look.

℅ stood there in the green not moving.

I thought whose horns were leaves.

I saw eight branches coming from whose head.

℅ didn't stop my looking.
℅ didn't run away.

I watched the whole of whose.

I saw whose arms and the taper of whose legs.

℅ let me watch whose for maybe hours

but really moments like a gift.

Like when you're almost home and smell them cooking supper

but you're still outside and could just
turn back around.

We stood like that together. ℁ let me touch the whole of whose.

Every rise and muscle.

℁ let me rest on the hollow of whose
neck and breathe it in   for four whole breaths.

℁ said my name or ℁ shook whose head inside
the leaves and sighed and let the light

come into us.   ℁ lets the light

hold us for awhile.

Major General,

Dad gets sleepy
and says my Brother will never
come back. He says it
as his hand falls off

his drink. *Pasadena's gone,*
Little Bird. We got the letter
where he said they call him
the name of where we're from.

I see him in the freeway
signs and at the bank.
I see him at the post office
and the high school pool.

Pasadena, I say. He says,
Little Sis, It's not so bad out
here. They gave me a new name.
I scratch it in the ground

with a stick. It lasts until the rains
come then I scratch it again.
Dad says he's not coming home
and scuffs it with his foot

so the *P* flies off and the *a's* explode
to nothing. I start all over again.
I'll make a banner with it written
in bright letters. *Pasadena!* Like a firework

show. Or a long day at the zoo,
all the flamingos running alongside us.
Like those football jackets
with his name blazing on the back.

Let yourself get loose and double.

It's funny how ℅ says that too.

We're in bed or we're lying

on the lake when I start

talking, worrying some thing

and ℅ says, *Shhh just let yourself get loose*

and double. What does that mean

to whose? I guess to let go. To let whose in.

We're in bed or we're lying on the wooden raft,

light coming to us in waves. I say,

The war into whose shoulder like a question

like a kiss so that ℅'ll stop me before I

start to say it but can tell myself I tried.

The word makes my lips open enough

to feel the warmth on whose skin.

The question makes them close

as ℁ turns over saying *You want to do it here?*

It means out there, the light

a visitation, the raft bobbing before we've started moving.

℁ says, *Let's talk about the war*

No. I want the other thing:

loose and double like the light does

on some stranger's raft I want

to do the other thing. To see us

blossom so we're four so %'s two

above me while the green spreads like wings.

Achingly Beautiful How the Sky Blooms Umber
at the End of the Day, Through the Canopy

Summers spent practicing in the apartment
stairwell: hand on the bannister, one foot after
another. Did I ever tell you I couldn't walk

until I was three and then sort of dragged
myself up and downstairs until I was seven
or eight? That burgundy carpet.

I'd stop to breathe and look out the window,
over brick tenements, toward the Capital
building. Oak leaves so full of late summer

sun even I thought, *Obscene,* and stood stunned
for a moment. My God. The urge to rest like the birds
on the phone wires, chatting like barristers

at the end of the day. Myself the useless
Ambassador from the third floor. I was the last one
up so the door was left open. I can still see it gaping

from two stories down. Sometimes music played.
Sometimes I'd smell supper. Neighbors stopped
to say hello. Achingly beautiful how the sky

looked as I stood after they left. Nicer somehow
in the middle. All the trees tucking blackbirds
into their darkness. It really did take this long.

Locked away we're like a Russian novel:

the hermit and the cowboy,

me stepping from the train.

A world of snow. Whose Great Coat a den

of baby foxes skinned and sewn together.

We're a field of stars,

all the peasants' sheep shorn in haste

made into a carpet placed beneath my feet,

the stationmaster's son sent through the night to find us

this small room.

℀'s the foxes and the wolves.

℀'s the doves with their curved necks

waiting out the rain. 𝄪's the grass

starting to shake. 𝄪's the medals

on whose own bureau, the silver

glinting on whose horse's bridle.

I said, *Samovar sounds like a knight.*

It's just a fancy tea pot. 𝄪's my samovar,

the steam that makes my cheeks glow

so all the women talk. 𝄪's the snow

covering the wolf's tracks,

the party of sleds sent out and not returning.

𝄪 gives me whose alphabet of notes

It's not all bad, I mean we laugh out here. Usually at T. who lets us laugh and makes us laugh at him. He's got this face like something in a book like with little mountains on it and one of his eyes kind of sticks out and he makes it stick out and he does the craziest things. He'll sort of prance around and wiggle his hips like a girl and when some guys are sleeping after getting drunk he'll wander up to them and lean down and blow a little in their ear. You'll hear them start to grin a little in their sleep, like sigh a bit and he'll put his fingers in their hair or he'll get a girl to come and do it if we're somewhere in town and she'll ask him what she should do and he'll start saying all these things. And we're just sitting there, cracking up and sometimes feeling shocked at the things that he comes up with. But it's true we all want those things. It's nice. And sometimes we'll just be sitting there so bored and T. will come back having found some cards or some radio turns up. He's good with wires and things and can make anything broken start up again. The first day I got here he said, *You need anything fixed you just call,* and then he winked and said, *And I can break most anything you want broken too.* He can. He can break things like you wouldn't believe. Which sometimes you need. And he seems to always be there knowing when and what you want to ask.

I like it when ℀ touches me there, right above the forehead

with whose whole palm and moves whose

hand along my skull until it rests below my neck,

and sort of holds me there. And how we stay

like that before it even starts right there in the stillness like the best part

of the movie when the lights go down and

everyone sort of shakes together and relaxes.

I like to watch whose start to want things right

before ℀ tells me what ℀ wants, how ℀

wants it before ℀ sighs and says my name

like a surprise

and starts to move whose hips. And how

℁ asks me how I do it, Oh God how

right there like that in the stillness

℁ sounds just like a girl

just like I sound when we come

together then relax. I like it

when whose hand tightens on my skull, right

at the place my neck begins. ℁ says

Sorry, I didn't mean to hold so tight. I say

It's fine, I like it

when you hold me like that.

Out here it's okay to be nothing. Want nothing. You feel
ashamed for a second then it's time to get moving. *Get moving,* T. says.
Or was it, *Get loving?* I wanted to stay in bed inside the tent. To hear all
the people breathing like we do until the tent's a hothouse or the inside
of a rocket ship. It's okay to cry sometimes, which seems strange to say.
In the films they make you stop. Not out here. It's okay to shake and say
I don't know or *Please* again and again. Someone's hand will find you.
Someone will ruffle your hair. Have you ever had a person say *It's okay,*
softly to you in the darkness? Keep your eyes shut and say it to yourself
and imagine. A voice different than yours. Let the sun come up inside
your mind.

In a Landscape of Perpetual Springtime

If I remember the locust it's not because I was there.
If I remember the deer with her tongue in my hand,

well, it's just because I heard a song about it once.
Oh, you say the deer was in the forest by the glade

and I was just come up from the water?
How strange. I could have sworn I was at the drive-in

watching Cherry Valance tell Ponyboy he didn't see her
at all. Wealth. It was a locust I had once. Chariots and gardens

so deep you couldn't even see the pillars holding up the house.
Once my grandmother made a necklace out of locusts

without having to kill a single one. Now that is what I call being rich.
She walked through the garden and I heard it singing.

She said, *Just listen.* And I heard the world spin round her and rise up.
I barely remember it and it's all I ever think about.

This was in the season of masturbation in the afternoon.
This was in The Age of the Guiding Light.

Which is to say: pure Decadence. One by one the locusts lined up
and snapped their brass jaws open: a battalion of soldiers

unbuttoning their great coats and baring their hearts.
Oh. It. Was. Beautiful. No metaphor will do.

My grandmother taking one of the hairs from the top of my scalp
and stringing it through. So slowly. I could see the locusts' flanks

heave in and out. The hair going in deeper until she pulled it out
the locust's backside. With her index finger and her thumb.

And moved onto the next one. Privilege. She brought the deer up.
They couldn't believe their eyes. And when I said

I wanted it? I wanted the chain of locusts around my throat?
She came toward me through the garden. The mayflies rose up

from the pools and made of themselves her crown. How am I supposed
to understand this economy when my grandmother made of the deer

a retinue? When I've beheld locusts' legs swimming toward me
as she pulled the necklace taut and laid it on my neck?

She Ties My Bow Tie

What you thought was the sound of the deer drinking
at the base of the ravine was not their soft tongues
entering the water but my Love tying my bow tie.
We were in our little house just up from the ravine.
Forgive yourself. It's easy to mistake her wrists
for the necks of deer. Her fingers move so deftly.
One could call them skittish, though not really because
they aren't afraid of you. I know. You thought it was the deer
but they're so far down you couldn't possibly hear them.
No, this is the breeze my Love makes when she ties me up
and sends me out into the world. Her breath
pulled taut and held until she's through. I watch her
in the mirror, not even looking at me. She's so focused
on the knot and how to loop the silk into a bow.

The Bandleader calls it the Angel Position.

The what? I asked. *The Angel Position. Let me*

explain, the Bandleader says. No.

Let me show you. Down on whose knees.

℀'s below me. I'm in the window,

the ocean behind us, the fronds of the palm

like a crown and in the shadow like

wings. Where the curtains would be

hooked, my wrists instead. *I don't know,*

I said. ℀ says, *You'll like it.*

Naked with the sun warming my back.

Almost sunset. *You're orange*, the Bandleader

says. *You're getting like fire.* My shadow

getting larger than me. My crown of palms

Now my wings against the wall. And the stool

my bare feet stand on shaking when ℅ touches

it. *Don't touch it,* I say. *Don't touch it, you'll break*

my arms. You're an angel, the Bandleader says,

You'll love it. At first the glass feels cool on my back.

℅ leaves me like that to go get a drink. To answer

the phone. What must the whales think?

An angel in the window. Another girl splayed

blocked a little by the palm

Dad and I, we once went up to the mountains to look at the
stars just us and we walked what felt like miles and I said, *Are we there
yet* and he said *Not yet. Stop whining.* I was always whining around him
I guess though I don't remember and it was getting dark and cold and
I said, *I don't want to walk anymore* and he didn't even look back you
remember how he wouldn't even look back and he said, *Keep going* and
I said, *I don't want to go anymore.* And I stopped right there and he just
kept on until I couldn't see him not even his bright jacket that he'd wear
in the woods and so I sat there and it did get dark and then I wanted
to follow him but I was too scared I'd get lost. Can you imagine that he
didn't come back to see where I was? I looked up and could see the stars
just fine from there and the point had been to take me and I know this
doesn't surprise you at all but I was surprised. I covered myself with
leaves and I heard something in the trees and remembered that falcons
nested there I heard branches breaking and birds calling out, not falcons
but little birds so I knew the falcons must be hunting and also coming
home to nest so eating right where they slept. I remember it scared me
a lot and I wished you were there but no one was there and I wanted to
find him but where would I go so I just sat there surrounded by leaves
and looked up not even knowing what I saw but how bright it was and I
imagined the falcons falling asleep and fell asleep myself and was there
until morning where there was a note telling me to walk straight down
and he'd be in the car.

Major General,

Dad calls her the Dowager but I call her Aunt G.
Aunt G at the Polo Lounge. Aunt G drinking gimlets
by the pool. Aunt G asking about Babe even
though she's the only one who sees her that much
anymore. She wears ten rings. Seven on her
right hand, which Dad calls the Seven Stars.
They make the glass seem like it's going to crack.

She doesn't like me very much. I know it.
I'm not her kind of girl. I won't wear dresses
and when she placed the ring inside my hand
I just said, *No thank you.* Not even thinking
how rude that might sound. What would I do
with a ring like that? I've got my own stars
and she doesn't really want to give

me presents anyway. She gave Babe a car,
her dark brown Aston Martin. And she gave
my Brother a watch *to remember home by.*
She gave my Dad a look when he said, *He's
a good soldier.* Like he gave her something bad
to eat. She just shook her head and said,
I'll never understand what kind of man you are.

And then she said Dad would have that young boy's
blood on his hands. Which I don't understand.
Or why she said, *You've gone and lost the both
of them. You're your very own Pol Pot,* while looking
through her purse. It shone so bright it blinded
me. For a second I saw spots and couldn't focus
on the thing. One clear stone that caught the light

and made reflections on my glasses. I didn't want
it. I don't wear things like that. *Who are you?*
she asked, not in a mean way but like she truly
didn't know. And didn't really care. She took it back
and asked me if I'd talked to Babe and I said
I had not and no one else had either.
I said, *She's living in the hills,*

and she looked at the ring for a minute
and put it back in her purse.

Falcon in the trees, bobcat in the grasses,

the Hermit took us through the orchard

to see the white pomegranate.

I asked when they'd be ripe.

In the fall. *Past us*, I thought.

If the Bandleader cared it didn't show

though ℅ liked the Hermit

or the idea of the Hermit: *How much do you think?*

How much does a hermit cost, all through dinner,

and how we couldn't take the pomegranates home.

I asked if they'd get red and the Hermit said

no, they'd stay like this.

I asked, *Are they sweet?*

Sweeter. Then deeper

into the orchard until

I couldn't see the Bandleader anymore.

Just green everywhere and the Hermit's straw hat—

like the grasses on the ranch we stayed at not gold

but—I can't say. Something like gold.

I followed him in deeper, not missing the Bandleader

at all. He said, *Autumn's good.*

And I said, *You mean better?* All the greens around

us like stars the way they shimmered

almost wet with the sun but not. *No. Not better.*

Just good. I felt a little sick in all the green,

like right before a school play starts:

everyone huddled in the wings not nervous just

too close. I said, *I saw a bobcat in the grasses.*

To steady myself I touched the trunk,

which was cooler.

Mulberry the Hermit said, *That's a mulberry,*

ignoring the bobcat, which the Bandleader

hadn't believed: *You didn't see a bobcat.*

The hermit said, *I did. I know it was. A bobcat*

lives around here,

and put a berry in my hand. The Bandleader

walking up to lean down

and take it in whose mouth.

Fox

What I thought was a vampire was nothing less than a fox
standing on the porch ledge after scratching at my door.

What I thought was the vampire on the television screen
I'd turned off to go to sleep was just the mother fox looking

for her babies who had congregated at the glass door that
the turkey stood by during the day as I read my Russian

novels. I wasn't scared of the scratching when I thought
of the vampire that might be standing at the door but I did lock

the door and then stepped away when I heard what I thought
was the vampire step away. I was curious so I went

into the bedroom and crawled onto my mattress so I could
lift the white blind that formed a kind of headboard as it kept

the light of morning out until I was ready. Fox.
there is no plainer way to say it. Fox.

Standing on the porch ledge looking at the door I'd just locked.
Fox looking at the sound of the lock turning. We were one

in our wondering. Which is not to say we were connected
or that she was mine in any way. Mother fox looking

at the sound of my unease. I forgot about the vampire,
about the baby foxes around the corner of the house.

She seemed to have too. Fixed as her black eyes were on the door.
Curious, her fur silver through the tail which bushed out

so that I thought of the novel I was reading with its sleigh rides
and balls. All the women wearing fox fur round their necks,

pushing their pale hands into the silver fox fur muffs as the sleigh
went faster. It really was this long: the time between us,

though she didn't notice me at all so focused was she on my ghost
in the other room.

Major General,

We used to love to dance. All of us together
out in the back yard. We'd turn on the radio
and not even care what was playing. Dad
liked oldies and my Brother did too. Babe would
roll her eyes but before you knew it she'd
be dancing. And sometimes we'd turn on
country music because my Brother liked it best,
Dad saying, *I don't know where you get*
that from. And Babe would say, *Yeah, partner,*
where'd you get that from? and she and Dad
would laugh together and then he'd spin her
around.

      I didn't mind it though. I liked what my Brother called
that twang. Like when you slam the screen door hard
and it rings so you feel it in your back teeth. *Like an orange,*
he would say, *but also sad.* "There's a Tear in My Beer"
and men named things like Merle. Sometimes I'd find him
listening all alone on that transistor Dad bought him
that that took him half a year to pay back. He always let me
sit by him. He'd hang his head down between his arms
like a cannonball and sort of cock it to the right so
the music could just pour in. I'd do it too not making fun
like Dad did when he was *just joking around* but so we
were two sitting there in the green.

You see? He'd say. *You see?* Most days I could not 'til
he explained it. What the song meant. How it made him
feel. Major General, my Brother is so kind. He's
the boy who walks you home from school no matter how
much younger you might be. He likes the sad songs
and the rowdy ones too. He likes to swing me around

even when his girls and all his friends come by. He says
just one second his dance card is full and turns the dial
up and takes me by the hand. *You're no kind of man,*
is what Dad says when he walks by so everyone can hear.
He takes my Brother's girlfriend by the hand and says,
Let's do a two step. Let me show you how it's really done.

℀'s really beautiful. When ℀'s standing in the trees
and thinks nobody sees whose. ℀'s like a stag.
Which sounds silly but ℀ is. The way the light shines

on whose. The way it bounces off whose hair
like spray from the sprinkler. And ℀ doesn't know.
Because ℀'s looking somewhere else.

Maybe up at a bird?   I was standing
and turned back because I heard
                    whose whistling.

℀ thought I wasn't listening.
                    ℀ wasn't thinking of me.
℀ was looking at a bird

who was sitting in the tree
and looking back at whose.
                    If whose shirt was off ℀'d

have been dappled golden by the sun
coming through the leaves. ℀ didn't notice me
watching whose without whose shirt on.

                    ℀ was standing in the forest
                    and the sun was coming
                    through the trees and covering whose.

℀ glowed.
I knew ℀'d be warm if I walked up and
touched whose. And probably not mad.

                    ℀'s like something in a movie
                    or like a book we'd read in summer by the pool.

⅚ didn't see me looking
because ⅚ was so peaceful
staring at the bird.

If I wait long enough I'll hear them nesting and I don't have to wait that long. They aren't scared of me: the falcons. I'm standing in the field beneath the trees and I can hear their wings before I see them. They come up from behind. They sound just like a helicopter starting. The slow turning, which is just their wings getting ready to coast. I hear them in my bones. It's true. I hear them in my spine like the little birds must. And it stills me. They don't care. They aren't afraid of me. I was standing in the field and I felt them coming one after the other and then they were above me. They flew into the trees. I heard the breaking. I heard the branches breaking. The sky was white like winter in the mountains. Or just before. It was like the fall when we'd go camping and the blue would turn to white. It was like their wings had turned it white. I looked and saw their heads. I saw their necks. They were thinner there in the trees. I could hear them settling in the darkening branches. I could hear them not being afraid of me.

I Had a Mane Once

A glorious thicket. A generosity
for all the cicadas to visit
when the rains descended.

I let the hornets make a mockery
of me. I didn't sweat it.
I let them sting and sting.

Because I was enormous
and magnanimous I cut my leg
and let the maggots build an Empire.

What did I care? I'd say to the fox,
There's enough meat in me
to go around. Then I'd stretch

so the grubs could find new avenues.
And they'd shiver with gratitude.
They'd pass out drunk along the edges

of the wound. I was my own
economy. You could see me coming
from miles around. And yes,

I could break your last best thing in half.
And yes, I was every inch an animal.
But most days I was merciful:

I'd pretend I was sleeping. I'd take all my danger
and lay it at the river's edge.

I was on all fours

and the sky was orange

I was on all fours looking out the window

the sky was orange

Turn around, the Bandleader said

and I said, *No.* I said I wanted to be

on all fours because the sky was orange I wanted

to see it set: the sun set. ℀ said

Turn around. I said, *Do you tell those other girls to*

turn around? ℀ said, *Turn around.*

I wanted to watch the sky turn darker,

to see if it would turn red. I said. *No.* I said

I want it like this.

Then ℀ said, *Turn your head around.*

The sky was on fire through the window

my arms were taut and orange in the light. I said

I don't want it like this.

(If I listened I could hear the falcons in the trees

loud and breaking the branches.) I wasn't

even wet anymore. I was watching. I said,

I can hear the falcons.

℀ said,

Turn around.

The fire fading. The room darkening between us.

The Good Guy's Got No Chance, It's Sad

In the face of the azalea breaking open
or in the case of the face being broken
open. He's got no chance. None at all.

Take your average person at the start
of spring. Winter's gone on forever.
Dear God you're sick of every patch of ice:

you fell at the top of the hill and punched
the ground until your knuckles bled
right through your gloves. Who cares

what kind of child you looked like?
The economy of winter'd worn you down.
You couldn't stand a single moment more,

not one. You'd tried: Optimistic as a dachshund
you made your way to work, the clouds
like mashed potatoes on a plate!

You didn't let the market get you down.
Let it dip. Let it crash into the gullies (so you said).
In the face of empty bank accounts

you bought the world a sandwich.
The last apple in the larder. Fool.
What did the fox whisper

when you walked into the darkness?
They'll eat your heart for breakfast.
Did you think it was a dream?

⌘'s really beautiful when ⌘ thinks no one is looking.

                                When ⌘ thought I wasn't looking

⌘ jumped up like a stag and spread whose arms out

                                in the orchard. We were walking

with the hermit. I started to laugh, I went to join

                                whose. The hermit took my arm,

he said, ⌘ *doesn't know you're looking.*

                                When ⌘ doesn't know I'm looking

⌘ stands stock still and smiles

                                ⌘'s really beautiful

when ⌘ thinks ⌘'s like an eight-point

                                stag standing in the orchard. I want

to take whose arm which would be warm and golden and

                              best before ⅝ feels me looking

and turns back to me and frowns.

Major General,

My eyes are shaky and glimmer like the stars.
My head turns to the left and it moves
just like a pendulum. The kids laugh and shake
it back to me, all the ways I'm stupid,
not like them. But I know how the grass sounds
when the locusts come, like a spaceship
taking off and how it makes the air shake.

Major General, I heard it in the branches
and the leaves. I heard the rocket leaving.
My teacher said it wasn't so, that it's
past hearing but my father said I could.
He puts his hands hard on my shoulders
from behind and holds my head still
with his looking. But I can feel how much

I want to shake and let myself go loose
and double like a cloud of mayflies on the lake,
you know just how they rise so you couldn't
see just one of them, not even with your thumb
held up to catch one with your eyes. It's something
I can't do that Babe and my Brother can, can't sight
the stars or use a telescope or ever fire a gun.

Major General, I like to think you're spinning
and can't feel it like I can't feel the world shake
unless I'm really tired and then it's like a gift
to let it go and just stop trying so hard. I like
to think you let go too and when the kids
run at me and move their heads from left
to right and call me Zigzag, I look up

and wish myself up there with you
just calm and swinging through the dark.

I like it when ⚥ touches me there, right above the forehead
with whose whole palm and moves whose hand along my skull until it
rests below my neck and sort of holds me there. We were out on point
and it got so cold that I don't know but I just sort of broke, just started
crying like Dad said I would when I told him I was going. Remember
how he told me I'd break? Well, I broke. But not how I'd have thought.
We weren't even in much danger and God knows by that time I'd seen
worse. But it was just cold and before I knew it I was crying in my stupid
hands and couldn't, just could not stop shaking and T. took his hand
and held it there, right there above my forehead and said *Shhhh* and
moved it over to the back but with this kind of pressure that made me
feel like I was getting still. I felt the earth beneath me and heard a train
off in the distance and said, *I'm sorry. I'm so fucking stupid,* and he said,
Don't worry, Pasadena. And just held my head there in his palm.

𝄋 said, *I want you in my mouth,*

                              on top. I got on top. I'd never

done that before. I got on top.

                              I lowered myself. Whose mouth

was waiting. I said, *Oh my God.*

                              I said, *Oh my God*:

I said, *Oh my God,*

                              your mouth is in me.

But that's not right—

                              I was covering the Bandleader's mouth

I said, *Oh my God*

                              I'm covering your mouth.

℁ pulled my hips down harder as if

to shut me up. So I was nothing

but the mountains outside with the Bandleader's

tongue inside me. I said, *Oh my God,*

I was nothing but the sky except inside I was nothing

but inside I said, *Don't stop.* ℁ rocked

my hips to shut me up.

I said, *I want it.*

I said, *I want it.*

℁ said, *Oh God.*

Shut up.

T. says it's fine because they don't understand the things
we're saying. T. says, *They don't know* as he ambles over to them. I
think they look just like the girls at home. He says, *Where are you from,
Pasadena?* Pasadena. I know it's different but I think they look the
same. After the rains how they step outside and put their hands above
their eyes to shield the sun. She does that when she steps outside. And
how they wave to each other when we're not all over them. Or even
when one's sitting on T.'s lap, how she waves at her friend walking
past ignoring T. for a second. He doesn't stop but it's like he's not
there putting his hand up her shirt and laughing and calling her . . .
well, calling her things I can't get myself to say. He says, *Call her little
_____*. He says, *Take her from behind and _____*. They look
like the girls at home. You'd see. How once one shook him off just like I
would do to Dad. And he beat her just the same.

Major General,

Shaky Eyes Horton had nystagmus too.
That's what my father said and took me
to the record store so we could buy him
and take him home to listen. Babe says
he's so square but we go all over. We listen
to music for hours and dance around
the house like crazy skeletons: loose

with all our bones knocking, we go,
click click click and wave our arms
and shake until we rattle all the china
in mom's cabinet. Dad turns the volume
up. We spin like planets round the sun.
Babe says he's no fun but I know different
because I see him laughing and I try,

which she just never does. She walks
into the house with some friend waiting in the car.
She grabs some clothes or asks for money,
though she doesn't even come to do that
anymore. They don't even talk. Last time
we had the music on loud and we were dancing.
I was letting my head swing back and forth

and she just stood and watched us with the strangest
look and I said, *I'm Shakey Eyes! Come dance!*
and moved my arms around. I followed her up
the stairs, swinging like a satellite and going,
ooh ooh ooooohhhhh just like a lowdown good-
for-nothing so-and-so. I know she thinks I'm funny
but she didn't laugh and I said, *Come dance!*

You know you've got the blues. She said,
You don't know him like I do.

Some Thoughts on Building the Atom Bomb

I would not have been great at it.
Firstly, I was terrible at science.
I got as far as slicing the frog's abdomen
open. Then I made an excuse
and walked the halls 'til the bell rang.

I know what you're thinking.
That's Biology. When I looked inside
the cavity I knew I didn't have what
it took. For a life in science. God,
I have intestines like that frog. They pulse
and shine like his. Cut me open,

you'll see my supper too. No.
When I looked inside the cavity
I thought, *I can't go on.* Volition.
That's a thing I don't have. I'd
leave the patient on the table
rather than get the job done.
I'd walk right into the desert

and roll around like a chinchilla
while everyone else back at the office
is considering implosion. *I'm dusty
as a chinchilla!* I'd say, entering the lab.
I'm the outside of your Mama's fallout shelter!
Those poor scientists. Every last one
wondering what I'm doing there.

I mean. I'd love to see the sky bloom
but I can do that already. Look!
the sky's blooming right now

outside the window. And plenty
of people are dying in various ways.
And won't the infrastructure fail
all on its own? Without me building

a bomb in the desert? These are the
kinds of questions that make me know
I'm not fit to decimate the planet.
Which is sort of sad to think
about. All that potential I'm just
giving up on.

I like the twang and sometimes we can hear it on the radio or
some guy gets a tape from home from his small town. Merle Haggard or
Conway Twitty. It cuts through the choppers and the smells. It brings
the women 'round to listen. I brought my radio from home, the one I
mowed lawns for all those months, remember? That transistor makes me
more friends than you can know. I go off by myself to listen and before
you know it there's a crowd telling me to find something better, not that
stupid country stuff some soul or R&B some rock and roll. But some
guys love it and tell me about their towns and how they listen at the
general store. Like Carolina, which may sound kind of girly except he's
huge and humps harder and faster than any of us. T. doesn't like him
much but I do. We just sit and sing the songs together and laugh. He has
this high voice that he just belts across the camp. I mean it's like one of
those Vienna Choir boys that Dad loves so much. He could not care less.
Just sings "Stand By Your Man" until everyone is rolling or until some
girl comes and takes him by the hand. They love him with his high
voice not caring who hears him sing.

Four Long Years At Court

I really miss the forest. And how
I used to hide there with the Queen.
I miss how we used to dance
and how we'd run from Court.

I miss the buttons (oh, her buttons),
how they'd shine in the late light
when she wasn't looking at me
arriving in the thicket—

where she'd somehow gotten first.
I wish she'd step down for the first time
again to greet me. In the great hall
where all the beasts' heads hovered.

All the torches lit her from within.
I was looking at the white bat cup the buck's rack,
swinging in the firelight like a lantern.
I saw its bones. Saw the fingers

hook onto to the antler. There she was.
Beside me. Watching me not see her.
You look to your right and time becomes
a torch blown huge. It was like that.

The bat looked like an otter's stomach
blown into a lamp. I told her so.
The way you will. If I had turned away.
Toward the ladies dancing. Toward

the door and walked out to the courtyard.
Toward the axes lined in rows and clean.
I miss how we'd walk into the clearings
and the caves. The deer walked up from the ravines

and stared. I wasn't scared of them or me
even with the things I'd done. Not when
she was there. I was so enamored
of the bat. Swinging. I could see its body

through the thin shroud of its wings.
I thought, *I could kill it with one hand.*
There she was. Watching me think it.
Watching me shake the thought of other

things into the darkness of the hall.
She touched my shoulder. Did I sing?
Sometimes to myself. Sitting by the river
or in the night to keep me safe. Sometimes

my name softly to myself to remind me.
Once beside my mother who'd swelled
to the size of a sheep. *The deer
is in the thicket. The fox is in the glade.*

Like that 'til she stopped breathing
and after as I watched the women
wash her. Not scared anymore,
neither one of us. I told her so.

How I sang. Of the fox and of the deer.
She held me in the clearing.
We could see the Towers
from there. It feels so long ago

and also like yesterday. Stepped down
from her throne and then together
in the forest. That fast and also
through the hours beside the King.

Turn toward me. I'd think it as she sat.
Turn. All the beasts' heads waiting.
The boars' mouths open. The lynx
with its pink tongue. The deer,

the deer, the deer one after another
on the walls. The hinds and harts.
The ten point stag I took down
as a mercy after the King missed

its chest seven times. I killed him
as he tried to crawl away. I sang
Stop. Sang, *The deer is in the thicket*
as his eyes rolled. *The fox is in*

the glade. I took his antler in my left
hand and pulled back, *Hey lolly lolly,*
pulled back until he groaned. I miss
the moment before it started,

the body just a figment, the deer
nothing but a song I sang beside
my mother as she died. It can
take forever. You can make a life

up in the time it takes to watch
your mother die. I was in the glade,
no I was in the bedroom, no
I was nowhere in the story.

Was nowhere to be found. I want
her back. I want the castle
and the bat. I even want the stag
who couldn't make up his mind

if he should die or not. If he should
let me pull his neck back. Or not.
Get loose and double, I'd sing
alone in my room or on the train

or as I walked to work. The world
around, a tapestry. I'd cock my head,
I'd see the stag. I'd cock my head,
I'd see the men in business suits.

I miss the Queen. I want her here.
Beside me. The null point's like a glade
where she'd lay me down beside
the stream. The beetles' armies

resting on the rocks. The Towers
in the distance. Your friends are with you
then they're gone. Your mother's with you
then she's gone. My armor shone

all morning, by nightfall it was blood and ash.
Hey lolly lolly. The fox is in the glade.
The debt collectors and the cans of soup.
One minute you're a castle. The next

you're just a cloud. Turn around.
Turn around in the late light.
If I cock my head I see the armies.
I could have walked from Court

and just kept going. Did I sing?
Ask the fox or the stag with his neck
pulled back. I want it back.

Null Point

The first thing I learned was to look wide
at the darkness

and not want anything. He'd say, *Just look*
at the darkness

and tell me what you see. I'd say, *I see stars* or
Just the stars, Dad.

And he'd say, *Don't call them that yet. What do you see?*
Just the stars, Dad.

But then I'd be quiet and let my eyes go and look wide
at the darkness.

It was like a dome. I think it frightened me to stare
at the darkness.

I see light. I see a million little lights. And he'd say
They aren't all stars.

Some were planets and some were planes and I'd say, *Yeah,*
they aren't all stars.

But not really believe it. But say it so not to feel stupid out there
in the darkness.

Dry Season at the End of the Empire

Oh, yes the chariots were everywhere that summer.
Running the wide streets and kicking up dust.

No rain for weeks. That's what we all said. No rain.
In drawing rooms. In parlours. At the card table

in The Dowager's Palace, which was just some rooms
she kept at the hotel. Oh, the last days of Empire

when no one quite wants to go home. So dry! All the trees rattling
when the wind blows from the desert. Like bones, she'd say.

Like a dance hall full of skeletons. We played bridge
at the end of the Empire. The bowls were always full of almonds.

Fields and fields of almonds for us to dip our hands into
and take. Everything growing somewhere. Everything ours.

I am so bored, somebody would say. So bored.
Rattle. Rattle of the ring in the bridge mix. Rattle of leaves outside.

Once a red bird sat at the window and we all tried to name it,
when we knew full well it was a cardinal.

Major General,

The Dowager makes tomato sandwiches
when I go to her house. We sit in the dining room
and Beverly brings them out, wearing her clean
dress that's as white as the bread.

She cuts the crusts off. Beverly does. I say,
Thank you for making these to the Dowager
who makes the strangest face and just says,
Eat. We only eat them in summer

even here in California where tomatoes
grow all year. We eat them on china plates
at the long dining table with one of us at either end.
One time I tried to sit beside the Dowager. She stared

at me 'til I got up and walked the long walk
to the other end. *We do things properly here,*
she said. And took a bite. I like it just the same,
the quiet as we eat. And how the tomato has that tang

when it mixes with the mayonnaise. Some days
Beverly brings me two and winks when the Dowager says,
You spoil her and mutters something about fat.
I'm not sure why she has me come except to ask about my father

or maybe Babe. Once I asked her about my Brother,
if she thought he was brave. She got up then
and said, *I think it's a long way to go to get away.*

I like to watch whose start to want things:

ice cream, an apple, some small star

we can just make out through the window

That's Cassiopeia. No. Andromeda? No.

It is! It's Cassiopeia! It makes me laugh.

I like to watch whose start to want the things

⅘ can't have. How ⅘ starts to stare

then smiles like no one's looking, whose eyes getting black

and wet like a horse.

And how whose head turns a little to the left and up a bit

as ⅘ sees whoself not having it

and hisses through whose teeth

like steam, like a smile

and I start laughing, which makes whose mad 'til ⅚ starts

laughing and says, *What?* and I say,

Nothing. Come here.

It *is* Andromeda.

No it's not. It just isn't.

I like to watch whose start to want things

that aren't some girl or some car.

The Bandleader on whose stomach,

staring out the window.

It *is*. As I kiss the small of whose back.

It's a long way to go to get away. That's for certain. I know. And to have come here on my own. I know. Most people think I'm crazy. Why not sign up for an office job or somewhere, well, somewhere not here. *How bad must your father be?* They wonder. *How stupid are you?* As we try to get our boots clean, as the rain pools around us, as the dogs in town won't come close because of how we smell. I was cleaning my gun and someone said, *Goddamn G., you're not fit for anything besides using that pretty face.* Why'd I come here? Why all the way out here? I watched Carolina walk towards me, holding his gun then squatting down. *Like this,* he said. *We're gonna do it together.*

"I was popular in certain circles"

among the river rats and the leaves,
for example. I was huge among the lichen,
and the waterfall couldn't get enough
of me. And the gravestones?
I was hugely popular with the gravestones.
Also with the meat liquefying
beneath. I'd say to the carrion birds,
I'd say, *Are you an eagle? I can't see*
so well. That made us laugh until we
were screaming. Eagle. Imagine.

The vultures loved me so much they'd feed
me the first morsel. From their delicate
talons, which is what I called them:
such delicate talons. They loved me so deeply
they'd visit in pairs. One to feed me.
One to cover my eyes with its velvety wings.
Which were heavy as theater curtains. Which I was
sure to remark on. *Why can't I see what I'm eating?*
I'd say. And the wings would pull me into
the great bird's chest. And I'd feel the nail
inside my mouth.

What pals I was with all the scavengers!
And the dead things too. What pals.
As for the living, the fox would not be outdone.
We'd sit on the cliff's edge and watch the river
like a movie and I'd say, *I think last night . . .*
and the fox would put his paw on top of mine
and say, *Forget it. It's done.* I mean,

we had fun. You haven't lived until a fox
has whispered something the ferns told him
in your one good ear. I mean truly.
You have not lived.

Some kids killed a goat and cooked him in the ground.

They had us over. Deep in the hills on someone

else's ranch. It was good.

They cooked him all day and asked us to come

by and ℀ loved it: the Bandleader

got out of the car laughing. It was good:

the kids ambling towards us lights making stars all around they said,

Come over!

The air smelled like smoke,

they lifted the goat out of the ground,

all their hands moving along it on the wood table. Seven knives and
everyone laughing. The kids picking off the skin and handing me some.
Then the ribs cut through. Then the haunches and the hams. Someone
took the head for soup. One of the older women. Someone brought
plates piled high with corn. *This is so good*, the Bandleader said. It came

right off the bone. We put it in tortillas and ate it with our fingers in the darkness with little lights shining above. It wasn't greasy like I thought it would be. Boys were feeding girls and laughing. Someone thanked the goat and all the sweet kids said, *Thank you, goat.* And the Bandleader said, *Thank you, goat* and grinned at me. All the kids running around and one ran up and said, *I know who you are!* And the Bandleader said, *Who am I?* And the boy squealed and ran away. *Come here,* I heard the Bandleader say. *Come here.*

⅜ feeding me the juiciest meat and kissing its steam off my chin.

You can hold a duck down on a rock and cut its head off.
You can hold a snake down on a rock and cut it in half and watch it keep lunging. You can cut a lizard like a green bean and the rock will turn a little green and then it'll turn black and the cats'll come to eat it. You can catch the cat and hold it down and cut its head off but it'll be harder because it knows you're coming and you'll have to know it knows you're coming and so it'll struggle so you'll have to not care anymore. You can kill it though. If you just let yourself get loose and double. That's what T. says, He says, *Get loose and double, Pasadena*. Meaning let one part of you go and let the other break its head with the stone you brought or maybe just get mad enough to crush its skull and let it lie there for a minute like a rag no other way to say it, like a rag. You can hold a monkey down and bash its skull in. You can look into its eyes and see it smile that smile at you that's not a smile and hear it hissing. You can feel its fingers grab your wrist but you can do it. You can. You can look it in the eye until it gets so still and stops thrashing. People back home say you can't, they say it will never stop fighting but everything stops fighting if you look at it right. That's what I told you. I said, *I can't fight him anymore,* and you said, *Yes, you can,* and now I can but that's because I'd know just what to do because I'd leave my body right beside me and slam his head down on the rock.

In the Darkness of the House of Pleasure

The Bandleader is indicative
of nothing or everything

depending on the day.
%'s boring and selfish.

%'s a Blue God.
Depending on the day

% brings me bouquets
of herbs %'s picked

while I was sleeping
or % forgets my name

entirely. What I call
Faith is also called

The Bandleader.
Sometimes we go

to the movies. Sometimes
we hold hands and eat

popcorn all the way
home. It's terribly

boring or it's the epitome
of joy. Depending.

Sometimes the canyons
echo through the windows

and I'm awake to hear it
because ℅'s kept me

sleepless with whose tongue.
Sometimes it's 4 am

and I don't know where
℅ is except I hear

whose laughter coming
from another house

where another girl
is wide awake.

Is the Bandleader a man?
A woman? Am I? These are questions

that don't matter to anyone.
Once the Bandleader

was Indigo and rising beneath
the mulberries. Once

I saw whose part the chest
of a stag and walk out from

inside, glistening and drunk
with light. Depending on the day

I am on my hands and knees
and begging for whose

or I am unsure if ℅ exists.
What art. ℅ is an elm

in every season and also
is the firmament. I count seven

stars between whose shoulder
blades and three inside

whose navel. And in whose eyes
I see nothing, they are so

dark they refuse whatever
light I offer. And yet. We lay

beside the stream on heated
stones and ℅ turned whose head

to look at me and I thought,
My Lord. This is love.

And yet. I have no proof.
Indeed that very night

℅ left me for a lion.
Once I watched whose

come toward me
for three whole blocks.

It's a thing I'll think
about forever.

Once I saw whose wear
a peach dress.

⅜ lit a rock on fire
in the depths of winter

as a testament to whose
fortitude. These are miracles:

the stone and the dress.
And the streets between

us that gave me time
to watch as ⅜ grew large

and still so delicate
before me. Some days

the phone is ravenous
with whose voice. Though now

it's mostly silent. The ranchlands
are given back to the hawks

where once we rode hard
to beat the train's passing.

It matters to no one
that the bouquet was made

of lemon balm, witch-hazel,
of rosemary with its bluest

flowers made manifest.
But I thought, My Lord.

And I thought
I would give anything.

Who Holds The Stag's Head Gets to Speak

Dear God who lives inside the stag's head
even after the stag's shot and lies slumped and abashed
on the forest floor. Protect him.

Even after he's been heaved onto the car's dark roof.
Forest Green. Or Pacific Blue. Nowhere he can see.
His body stiffens like a trellis above the driver.
Help him. Hold him in your sight.

I know the age of prayer is over. I read it on my newsfeed.
Someone said someone said someone said, *Faith is a weapon
of the Man.*

When they take him down in the darkness
he looks like any body. Could you rest the muscle of your breath
against his neck so he won't sag? So the man thinks he's alive
and quakes in the awful company of the risen.

You are the Blue Lord I prayed for when I was hunted.
You came to me through the branches. I could hear you
in the upper room where I had hidden in the cupboard.

The moment the blade goes to gut him please make of his entrails
a phalanx of butterflies. And of his lungs a great bear
charging. My Lord. When I was the cowered beast
you turned me clear as water so the Hunter could not find me.

I beseech you. Abide.

Praise House: The New Economy
—after and for Ross Gay

The rosemary bush blooming
its unabashed blue. Also dumplings
filled with steam and soup
so my mouth fills and I bubble
over with laughter. Little things.
People kissing on bicycles.
Being able to walk up the stairs
and run back down.
Joanna's garden after the long flight
to Tel Aviv. Not being detained
like everyone thought I would.
The man with dreadlocks
and a perfect green shirt walking home
from work. One cold beer
before I drink it and get sick.
How peaches mold into compost in a single day:
orange to gray to darkness into dirt.
Her ankle's taste. The skin
right under the knob, delicate
as a tomatillo's shroud. All the animals
that talk to me. That I finally let them
talk to me. The blessing of waking
early enough to watch the fox
bathe itself. The suction of a man's hands
meeting another's on the street.
Every single person looking up
to see them. Bros, yes. But lovely
in the golden light with brims swung
to the back. I want shoulders like
they have. Want my waist to taper
to an ass built like the David's. I admit it:
this body's not enough for me.

Still I love it. Al B Sure blasting
out a Nissan Sentra's windows.
Bowties. Ridiculous blues.
My mother's seizures—specifically
that I don't have them.
That I can answer Ross' call
or not because we live Harmonious
and are always talking somehow.
Tapestries with their gluttony of deer.
Fig perfume and also cypress.
Boxer briefs and packing socks
in jockey shorts. Strap ons.
Soft and hard. Welcome in her hand
and in mine as I greet the real me.
The little shop in Provincetown.
And the speckled dog that licks itself
in that fresco of the crucifixion.
Mary Oliver. I love her. I really do.
The baseball she gave me
that says, *Go Sox!* Though, I love
the Orioles. Old Bay on all my shrimp.
And justice. And cities burning
if people need to burn them to get free.
My grandmother gardening
in the late light. Sun Ra. The first time.
Paris, even though I've never been
there. Natal plums. Tattoos everlasting:
Clouds. Orion's belt. Pushing inside her
with both hands holding myself
up. My weight. Her grabbing and saying,
God. Fuck. The neighbors.
Casablanca. Not knowing anything.
Angels. Mashed potatoes. Good red wine.

The paint chipped away on the wall looked like the bull

that we found in the sky: little bull's legs

with the big head and a pile of stars in his neck.

Near the Queen's Suite

that rises in Autumn.

Pegasus, Andromeda, and The Great

Square. (what we called my father

when we got old enough,

before we didn't talk anymore)

Imagine having a pile of stars in your neck,

a bull made of stars.

I liked it best when we'd lie there

and look out the window.

I'd run my hand through the air and say,

There to there

to there. It doesn't really make sense

unless you know what you're looking for.

You know?

Little bull in the sky on the wall with it's hickey of stars.

Someone sucked the light right
to the surface.

Let me show you, I'd say.

Let me show where we are.